Cool African Cooking

Fun and Tasty Recipes for Kids

Lisa Wagner

TO ADULT HELPERS

You're invited to assist an up-and-coming chef! As children learn to cook, they develop new skills, gain confidence, and make some delicious food. What's more, it's going to be a lot of fun!

Efforts have been made to keep the recipes in this book authentic yet simple. You will notice that some of the recipes are more difficult than others. Be there to help children with these recipes, but encourage them to do as much as they can on their own. Also encourage them to try new foods and experiment with their own ideas. Building creativity into the cooking process encourages children to think like real chefs.

Before getting started, set some ground rules about using the kitchen, cooking tools, and ingredients. Most importantly, adult supervision is a must whenever a child uses the stove, oven, or sharp tools.

So, put on your aprons and stand by. Let your young chefs take the lead. Watch and learn. Taste their creations. Praise their efforts. Enjoy the culinary adventure!

visit us at www.abdopublishing.com

Published by ABDO Publishing Company, a division of ABDO, P.O. Box 398166, Minneapolis, Minnesota 55439. Copyright © 2011 by Abdo Consulting Group, Inc. International copyrights reserved in all countries. No part of this book may be reproduced in any form without written permission from the publisher. Checkerboard Library™ is a trademark and logo of ABDO Publishing Company.

Printed in the United States of America, North Mankato, Minnesota
102010
012011

♻ PRINTED ON RECYCLED PAPER

Design and Production: Colleen Dolphin, Mighty Media, Inc.
Art Direction: Colleen Dolphin
Series Editor: Liz Salzmann
Food Production: Frankie Tuminelly
Photo Credits: Colleen Dolphin, iStockphoto/Rainbowphoto, Photodisc, Shutterstock

The following manufacturers/names appearing in this book are trademarks: Clear Value®, Del Monte®, Gold Medal®, Heinz®, La Preferida®, Market Pantry®, Morton®, Pyrex®, Roundy's®, Target®

Library of Congress Cataloging-in-Publication Data

Wagner, Lisa, 1958-
  Cool African cooking : fun and tasty recipes for kids / Lisa Wagner.
    p. cm. -- (Cool world cooking)
  Includes index.
  ISBN 978-1-61714-658-9
  1. Cooking, African--Juvenile literature. I. Title.
  TX725.A4W34 2011
  641.596--dc22
                                    2010022190

Table of Contents

EXPLORE THE FOODS OF AFRICA! 4

THE BASICS 6

THE TOOL BOX 8

COOL COOKING TERMS 10

THE COOLEST INGREDIENTS 12

AFRICAN EXTRAS 16

SEASONED CHICKPEA SALAD 18

SIZZLING GROUNDNUT STEW 20

JUICY JOLLOF RICE 22

MOROCCAN CARROT SALAD 24

AUTHENTIC ALECHA 26

TROPICAL FRUIT SALAD 28

WRAP IT UP! 30

GLOSSARY 31

WEB SITES 31

INDEX 32

Explore the Foods of Africa

Africa is the second-largest continent. It has more than 50 countries. The people speak more than 1,000 different languages! There are also magnificent mountains, jungles, deserts, tropical rainforests, and miles of coastline.

Most Africans eat more fruits and vegetables than meat. Fish is **available** along the coasts. A lot of different fruits are grown in the tropical areas. Yams, rice, corn, onions, tomatoes, and chili peppers are common in hot, dry areas.

African cooking varies by region. In this book, we will explore recipes from Algeria and Morocco in the north, Ethiopia and Kenya in the east, and Ivory Coast and Liberia in the west.

Substitutions are common in African cooking. People cook with what is **available**! A creative cook can make a **delicious** stew with a few vegetables, a little water, and some spices! It's called **improvising**! Are you ready for a tasty African adventure? Put on your apron and off we go!

4

GET THE PICTURE!

When a step number in a recipe has a dotted circle around it, look for the picture that goes with it. The circle around the photo will be the same color as the step number.

4 →

HOW DO YOU SAY THAT?

You may come across some African words you've never heard of in this book. Don't worry! There's a pronunciation guide on page 30!

The Basics

Get going in the right direction
with a few important basics!

ASK PERMISSION

Before you cook, get permission to use the kitchen, cooking tools, and ingredients. When you need help, ask. Always get help when you use the stove or oven.

GET ORGANIZED

- Being well organized is a chef's secret ingredient for success!

- Read through the entire recipe before you do anything else.

- Gather all your cooking tools and ingredients.

- Get the ingredients ready. The list of ingredients tells how to prepare each item.

- Put each prepared ingredient into a separate bowl.

- Read the recipe instructions carefully. Do the steps in the order they are listed.

GOOD COOKING TAKES PREP WORK

Many ingredients need preparation before they are used. Look at a recipe's ingredients list. Some ingredients will have words such as chopped, sliced, or grated next to them. These words tell you how to prepare the ingredients.

Give yourself plenty of time and be patient. Always wash fruits and vegetables. Rinse them well and pat them dry with a **towel**. Then they won't slip when you cut them. After you prepare each ingredient, put it in a separate prep bowl. Now you're ready!

6

BE SMART, BE SAFE

- If you use the stove or oven, you need an adult with you.
- Never use the stove or oven if you are home alone.
- Always get an adult to help with the hot jobs, such as frying with oil.
- Have an adult nearby when you are using sharp tools such as knives, peelers, graters, or food processors.
- Always turn pot handles to the back of the stove. This helps prevent accidents and spills.
- Work slowly and carefully. If you get hurt, let an adult know right away!

BE NEAT, BE CLEAN

- Start with clean hands, clean tools, and a clean work surface.
- Tie back long hair so it stays out of the way and out of the food.
- Roll up your sleeves.
- An apron will protect your clothes from spills and splashes.
- Chef hats are **optional**!

KEY SYMBOLS

In this book, you will see some symbols beside the recipes. Here is what they mean.

HOT STUFF!
The recipe requires the use of a stove or oven. You need adult assistance and supervision.

SUPER SHARP!
A sharp tool such as a peeler, knife, or grater is needed. Get an adult to stand by.

NUT ALERT!
Some people can get very sick if they eat nuts. If you are cooking with nuts, let people know!

EVEN COOLER!
This symbol means adventure! Give it a try! Get inspired and invent your own cool ideas.

No Germs Allowed!

Raw eggs and raw meat have bacteria in them. These bacteria are killed when food is cooked. But they can survive out in the open and make you sick! After you handle raw eggs or meat, wash your hands, tools, and work surfaces with soap and water. Keep everything clean!

The Tool Box

Each recipe in this book lists the tools you will need.
These pages will help you learn about the tools you don't know!

SERRATED KNIFE

SMALL SHARP KNIFE

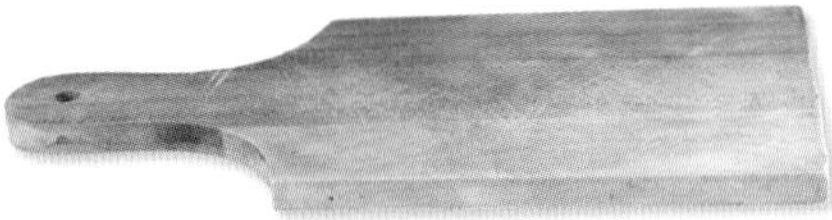

CUTTING BOARD

MEASURING CUPS

MEASURING SPOONS

LIQUID MEASURING CUP

PREP BOWLS

MIXING BOWLS

WOODEN SPOON

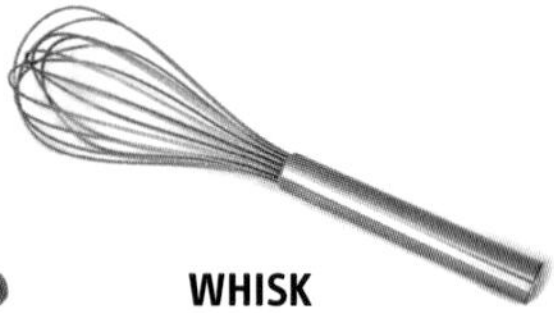

SPATULA

WHISK

CAN OPENER

FORK

PEELER

ROLLING PIN

PLATE

SAUCEPAN

POT HOLDERS

FRYING PAN

STRAINER

KITCHEN TOWEL

JUICER

HEAVY-BOTTOMED
SAUCEPAN

GRATER

SALAD BOWL

SLOTTED SPOON

TIMER

PLASTIC WRAP

9

Cool Cooking Terms

Here are some basic cooking terms and the actions that go with them. Whenever you need a reminder, just turn back to these pages.

FIRST THINGS FIRST

Always wash fruit and vegetables well. Rinse them under cold water. Pat them dry with a **towel**. Then they won't slip when you cut them.

CHOP

Chop means to cut things into small pieces with a knife.

CUBE OR DICE

Cube and *dice* mean to cut cube or dice shapes. Usually *dice* refers to smaller pieces and *cube* refers to larger pieces.

GRATE

Grate means to shred something into small pieces using a grater.

SAUTÉ

Sauté means to cook using a small amount of grease in a shallow pan over high heat.

WHISK

Whisk means to beat quickly by hand with a whisk or fork.

SLICE

Slice means to cut food into pieces of the same thickness.

MINCE

Mince means to cut the food into the tiniest possible pieces. Garlic is often minced.

KNEAD

Knead means to fold, press, and turn dough to make it smooth.

PEEL

Peel means to remove the skin, often with a peeler.

JUICE

To *juice* a fruit means to remove the juice from its insides by squeezing it or using a juicer.

The Coolest Ingredients

GREEN BEANS

WHITE ONION

POTATOES

SWEET POTATO

CARROTS

GINGER ROOT

ZUCCHINI

CABBAGE

GREEN BELL PEPPER

RED BELL PEPPER

SCALLIONS

OKRA

FRESH PARSLEY

FRESH CILANTRO

FRESH THYME

MANGO

GARLIC

BAY LEAVES

TOMATO

LEMONS

LIMES

PINEAPPLE

BANANAS

SALT

CAYENNE PEPPER

GROUND PEPPER

GROUND CUMIN

LONG-GRAIN RICE

PAPRIKA

SHREDDED COCONUT

TOMATO SAUCE

CANNED WHOLE TOMATOES

CANNED MIXED TROPICAL FRUIT

ALL-PURPOSE FLOUR

CHICKEN BROTH

CHICKPEAS

RED WINE VINEGAR

OLIVE OIL

CANOLA OIL

PEANUT BUTTER

CHICKEN BREASTS

Allergy Alert!

Some people have a reaction when they eat certain foods. If you have any allergies, you know what it's all about. An allergic reaction can require emergency **medical** help. Nut allergies can be especially **dangerous**. Before you serve anything made with nuts or peanut oil, ask if anyone has a nut allergy.

Salt and Pepper to Taste?

Some recipes say to add salt and pepper to taste. This means you should rely on your taste buds. Take a small spoonful of the food and taste it. If it isn't as salty as you like, add a little salt. If it needs more ground pepper, add some. Then mix and taste it again.

African Extras

Take your African cooking to the next level! The ideas on these pages will show you how.

CRUNCHY CABBAGE SALAD

Makes 8 servings

INGREDIENTS

½ cabbage, sliced very thin
3 carrots, peeled and grated
15-ounce can mixed tropical fruit, drained
juice from 1 lime
¼ teaspoon salt
3 tablespoons canola oil

1 Put the cabbage, carrots, and tropical fruit in a salad bowl. Mix well.

2 In mixing bowl, whisk the lime juice, salt, and oil together. Pour the mixture over the salad and mix well. Cover and refrigerate for an hour before serving.

PERFECTLY COOKED RICE

Makes 4 to 6 servings

INGREDIENTS

3 cups water
1½ cups long-grain rice
1 teaspoon salt

1 Combine water, rice, and salt in a saucepan. Bring to a boil.

2 Cover the pan when little holes appear between the grains of rice. This should take about 8 minutes. The surface of the rice will also look a little dry.

3 Turn the heat down to very low. Cook the rice for 15 more minutes.

4 Remove the pan from the heat. Let the rice stand, covered, for 5 minutes.

5 Fluff the rice with a fork before serving.

FANTASTIC CHAPATI FLATBREAD

Makes 4 chapati

INGREDIENTS

2 cups all-purpose
    flour
1 teaspoon salt
⅔ cup warm water
2 teaspoons canola oil

1 Put the flour and salt in a mixing bowl. Mix them with a fork.

2 Slowly add the warm water. Mix with your hands. Make sure you wash them first! As you mix, it will start to turn into dough. If the mixture doesn't become a thick dough, add 1 teaspoon of warm water. Then mix it some more. Keep adding warm water 1 tablespoon at a time. Mix well after each time. Stop when the dough is thick.

3 Mix in the canola oil.

4 Sprinkle some flour on a cutting board. Use only enough flour to keep the dough from sticking. Knead the dough until is a smooth ball. Put it in a bowl.

5 Cover the bowl with a clean kitchen **towel**. Let the dough rest for 30 minutes.

6 Divide the dough into four equal pieces. Shape each piece into a ball.

7 Sprinkle more flour on the cutting board as needed. Use a rolling pin to flatten each ball of dough. They should each be about 6 to 7 inches across. You can also flatten the dough by hand.

8 Put 1 teaspoon of oil in a frying pan. Heat over medium-high heat until the oil is hot.

9 Put one piece of dough in the pan. Fry it for 3 minutes on one side. Then flip the chapati with a spatula. Fry it for 3 minutes on the second side. Each side of the chapati should have golden brown marks on it. If the dough gets burned spots, turn down the heat.

10 Remove the chapati and put it on a plate. Cover it with a clean kitchen towel while you fry the next one.

11 Repeat Steps 8 through 10 until all the dough is fried.

Seasoned Chickpea Salad

A healthy and tasty Algerian dish chock full of flavor!

MAKES 6 TO 8 SERVINGS

INGREDIENTS

4 tablespoons olive oil

1 tablespoon red wine vinegar

1 tablespoon lemon juice

¾ cup finely chopped parsley

½ teaspoon salt

¼ teaspoon ground pepper

2 15-ounce cans chickpeas, rinsed and drained

1 white onion (about 3 inches across), minced

4 scallions, chopped

TOOLS: juicer, measuring cups, can opener, whisk, prep bowls, cutting board, strainer, wooden spoon, measuring spoons, small sharp knife, mixing bowl

1. Put the olive oil, vinegar, and lemon juice in a large bowl. Whisk them together. Add the parsley, salt, and pepper. Whisk to blend.

2. Add the chickpeas, onion, and scallions. Mix well with a wooden spoon.

3. Chill for at least 1 hour before serving.

Even Cooler!

Use ½ cup finely chopped cilantro instead of the parsley. Also add 1 teaspoon ground cumin.

Sizzling Groundnut Stew

A wonderful West African specialty for lunch or dinner!

MAKES 4 TO 6 SERVINGS

INGREDIENTS

1 white onion (about 4 inches across), chopped

2 tablespoons canola oil

½ teaspoon cayenne pepper

3 cloves garlic, minced

1 tablespoon ginger root, grated

4 cups vegetables, cubed (sweet potatoes, green and red bell peppers, zucchini)

2 cups liquid (chicken broth or water)

2 tomatoes, chopped

6 pieces okra, cut in ¼-inch slices

½ cup warm water

¾ cup peanut butter

15-ounce can chickpeas, rinsed and drained

salt

ground pepper

TOOLS:

measuring spoons
measuring cups
prep bowls
cutting board

serrated knife
small sharp knife
strainer
heavy-bottomed saucepan

mixing bowl
wooden spoon
whisk
can opener

grater
peeler
pot holders
timer

1. Put the onions and oil in a heavy-bottomed saucepan. Sauté for 5 minutes. Add the cayenne pepper, garlic, and ginger. Sauté for 2 minutes.

2. Add the vegetables and sauté for 2 more minutes.

3. Mix in the liquid and the tomatoes. Cover and **simmer** 10 minutes or until vegetables are tender. Add the okra and simmer 5 minutes.

4. Whisk ½ cup warm water and the peanut butter together until smooth. Add the peanut butter mixture to the pot and stir. Add the chickpeas and simmer for 10 minutes. Add salt and pepper to taste. Serve over rice.

Even Cooler!

For a more **authentic** meal, serve this stew with plantains. Use one plantain for each serving. Peel and cut each plantain into four pieces. Place them in a saucepan and cover them with cold water. Boil over medium-high heat until the plantains are tender. Drain them in a strainer. Put them in a bowl with 1 tablespoon of butter. Mash with a fork. Add salt and pepper to taste!

..... Tip .....

Peel the skins off the sweet potatoes before you cut them.

Juicy Jollof Rice

This excellent West African dish is a filling meal by itself!

MAKES 4 SERVINGS

INGREDIENTS

- 3 chicken breasts, cubed
- 1 white onion (about 4 inches across), diced
- ¼ cup canola oil
- 28-ounce can whole tomatoes
- 2 green or red bell peppers, diced
- 8-ounce can tomato sauce
- 1 bay leaf
- 1 teaspoon thyme
- 15-ounce can chicken broth
- 1 cup long-grain rice
- salt
- ground pepper

TOOLS:

measuring spoons	cutting board	heavy-bottomed saucepan	strainer
measuring cups	serrated knife	wooden spoon	pot holders
prep bowls	small sharp knife	can opener	timer
mixing bowls	slotted spoon		

Put the chicken and onion in a mixing bowl. Mix well using your clean hands.

 Heat the canola oil in a heavy-bottomed saucepan over medium-high heat. Add the chicken mixture. Stir the chicken so it gets browned on all sides. When chicken is browned, remove it using a slotted spoon. Put it in a bowl and set it aside.

3 Strain the juice from the can of tomatoes into a bowl. Chop the tomatoes into bite-size pieces.

4 Put the bell peppers and tomatoes in the saucepan. Sauté for 3 minutes. Add the tomato sauce, bay leaf, thyme, broth, rice, and chicken.

 Cover the pan. **Simmer** over low heat for 45 to 60 minutes until the rice is done. Stir every 10 minutes to keep the rice from sticking to the pan. If all the liquid gets **absorbed**, add ¼ cup water. Add salt and pepper to taste and serve.

Even Cooler!

For a more **authentic** flavor, add ½ teaspoon cayenne pepper. Be careful! This pepper is very hot. Do not sniff the pepper. Be sure to wash your hands if you touch it.

Moroccan Carrot Salad

This simple and delicious salad is easy to make and great to eat!

MAKES 6 TO 8 SERVINGS

INGREDIENTS

- 1 pound carrots, peeled and cut into ½-inch slices
- 3 tablespoons lemon juice
- 3 tablespoons olive oil
- 1 teaspoon paprika
- 2 cloves garlic, minced
- 1 teaspoon ground cumin
- ½ cup cilantro, finely chopped
- salt
- ground pepper

TOOLS:

prep bowls	peeler	mixing bowls	strainer
measuring spoons	small sharp knife	whisk	
measuring cups	4-quart saucepan	wooden spoon	
cutting board	juicer	timer	

1. Fill a 4-quart saucepan with water. Bring it to a boil. Add the carrots and cook for 5 minutes. Drain the carrots and let them cool. Put the carrots in a mixing bowl.

2. Put the remaining ingredients, except the cilantro, salt, and pepper in a small bowl. Whisk well. Pour the dressing over the carrots and mix.

3. Add the cilantro. Season with salt and pepper to taste. Mix well and chill.

Even Cooler!

For a spicier **version**, add ½ teaspoon hot pepper flakes or ⅛ teaspoon cayenne pepper.

Authentic Alecha

Make this Ethiopian veggie side dish spicy by adding hot peppers!

MAKES 6 SERVINGS

INGREDIENTS

- 6 small potatoes, peeled and thinly sliced
- ½ pound green beans, stems removed
- 4 carrots, peeled and thinly sliced
- ¼ cup canola oil
- 2 green or red bell peppers, thinly sliced
- 2 medium white onions, sliced into ½-inch crescents
- 1 tablespoon ginger root, grated
- 4 cloves garlic, minced
- 4 scallions, sliced
- salt
- ground pepper

TOOLS: prep bowls, measuring spoons, measuring cups, cutting board, small sharp knife, peeler, grater, strainer, 4-quart saucepan, heavy-bottomed saucepan, wooden spoon, pot holders, timer

1. Fill a 4-quart saucepan half full with water. Bring the water to a boil. Add the potatoes, beans, and carrots.

 2. Cover and boil for 5 minutes. Drain the vegetables in a strainer and rinse with cold water. Set them aside.

 3. Heat the canola oil in a heavy-bottomed saucepan. Add the peppers and onions. Sauté for 5 minutes. Add the ginger, garlic, scallions, and 1 teaspoon salt. Sauté for 5 minutes.

4. Add the drained vegetables and stir well. Cook over medium heat for 5 to 10 minutes. Stop when the vegetables are tender. Add salt and pepper to taste. Serve with rice or chapati.

Even Cooler!

For a spicier dish, add four Anaheim chili peppers. Prep these the same way you prep red or green peppers. Add them with the other peppers and onions. Like it even hotter? Add two sliced jalapeño peppers.

Tropical Fruit Salad

INGREDIENTS

3 bananas, peeled and cut into
  ½-inch slices

2 mangoes, peeled and cubed

2 cups pineapple, cubed

juice from 1 lime

½ cup shredded coconut

A delightful fresh fruit treat
that is great for a snack or dessert!

MAKES 8 SERVINGS

TOOLS: prep bowls   serrated knife   mixing bowl
cutting board   juicer   wooden spoon
small sharp knife   measuring cups   plastic wrap

Slice the bananas and cube the mangoes and pineapple.

2 Mix the bananas, mangoes, and pineapple together in a large bowl. Add the lime juice and mix well.

3 Cover with plastic wrap and refrigerate for 1 hour. Sprinkle with coconut just before serving.

Even Cooler!

Try other tropical fruits such as guava, papaya, or avocado. You can also use pear, peach, melon, apple, grapefruit, orange or tangerine. Add 1 tablespoon of chopped fresh mint when you add the juice.

Wrap it Up!

Now you know how to make **delicious** African dishes! What did you learn? Did you try any new foods? Learning about recipes from around the world teaches you a lot. You learn about different **cultures**, climates, geography, and tastes.

Making international dishes also teaches you about different languages. Did you learn any new words in this book? These new words will help you sound like a native speaker. You'll be able to use them at restaurants and **grocery stores**.

alecha (ah-LAY-chuh)

chapati (cha-PA-tee)

jollof (jaw-loff)

Glossary

absorb – to soak up or take in.

authentic – real or true.

available – able to be had or used.

culture – the behavior, beliefs, art, and other products of a particular group of people.

dangerous – able or likely to cause harm or injury.

delicious – very pleasing to taste or smell.

grocery store – a place where you buy food items.

improvise – to use what you have on hand to make something.

medical – having to do with doctors or the science of medicine.

optional – something you can choose, but is not required.

simmer – to stew gently at a soft boil.

substitution – the act of replacing one thing with another.

towel – a cloth or paper used for cleaning or drying.

version – a different form or type from the original.

Web Sites

To learn more about cool cooking, visit ABDO Publishing Company on the World Wide Web at **www.abdopublishing.com.** Web sites about cool cooking are featured on our Book Links page. These links are routinely monitored and updated to provide the most current information available.

Index

A

Adult help/permission, 6, 7
Africa
    description of, 4
    food/cooking in, 4, 30
Alecha, 26–27
Allergies, 15

B

Bacteria, 7

C

Cabbage salad, 16
Carrot salad, 24–25
Chapati, 17
Chickpea salad, 18–19
Chopping, 10
Cleanliness guidelines, 6, 7, 10
Cooking terms, 10–11
Cubing, 10

F

Flatbread, 17
Fruit salad, 28–29

G

Grating, 10
Groundnut stew, 20–21

I

Ingredients
    cleanliness of, 6, 10
    common types of, 12–15
    preparation of, 6
    substitution of, 4

J

Jollof rice, 22–23
Juicing, 11

K

Kneading, 11

L

Languages, learning about, 30

M

Mincing, 11

P

Peeling, 11
Permission, for cooking/kitchen use,
    6, 7
Preparation, for cooking, 6

R

Recipes, reading of, 6
Rice, 16, 22–23

S

Safety guidelines, 7, 15
Salads, 16, 18–19, 24–25, 28–29
Salt and pepper, 15
Sautéing, 10
Seasoning, 15, 19, 23, 25, 27
Slicing, 11
Stew, 20–21
Stove/Oven use, 6, 7
Substitution, of ingredients, 4

T

Tools
    cleanliness of, 7
    common types of, 8–9
    preparation of, 6

W

Whisking, 11